A wish for a soft landing to everyone
drifting with me through this life – L.N.

To my darling nieces, My and Ha – X.L.

A TEMPLAR BOOK

First published in the UK in 2025 by Templar Books,
an imprint of Bonnier Books UK
5th Floor, HYLO, 105 Bunhill Row,
London, EC1Y 8LZ
The authorised representative in the EEA
is Bonnier Books UK (Ireland) Limited.
Registered office address:
Floor 3, Block 3, Miesian Plaza
Dublin 2, D02 Y754, Ireland
compliance@bonnierbooks.ie
www.bonnierbooks.co.uk

Text copyright © 2025 by Lela Nargi
Illustration copyright © 2025 by Xuan Le
Design copyright © 2025 by Templar Books

1 3 5 7 9 10 8 6 4 2

All rights reserved

ISBN 978-1-80078-211-2

Edited by Carly Blake
Designed by Jeni Child and Laura Hall
Production by Nick Read
Consultant Camilla de la Bedoyere

Printed in China

MIX
Paper | Supporting
responsible forestry
FSC® C178225

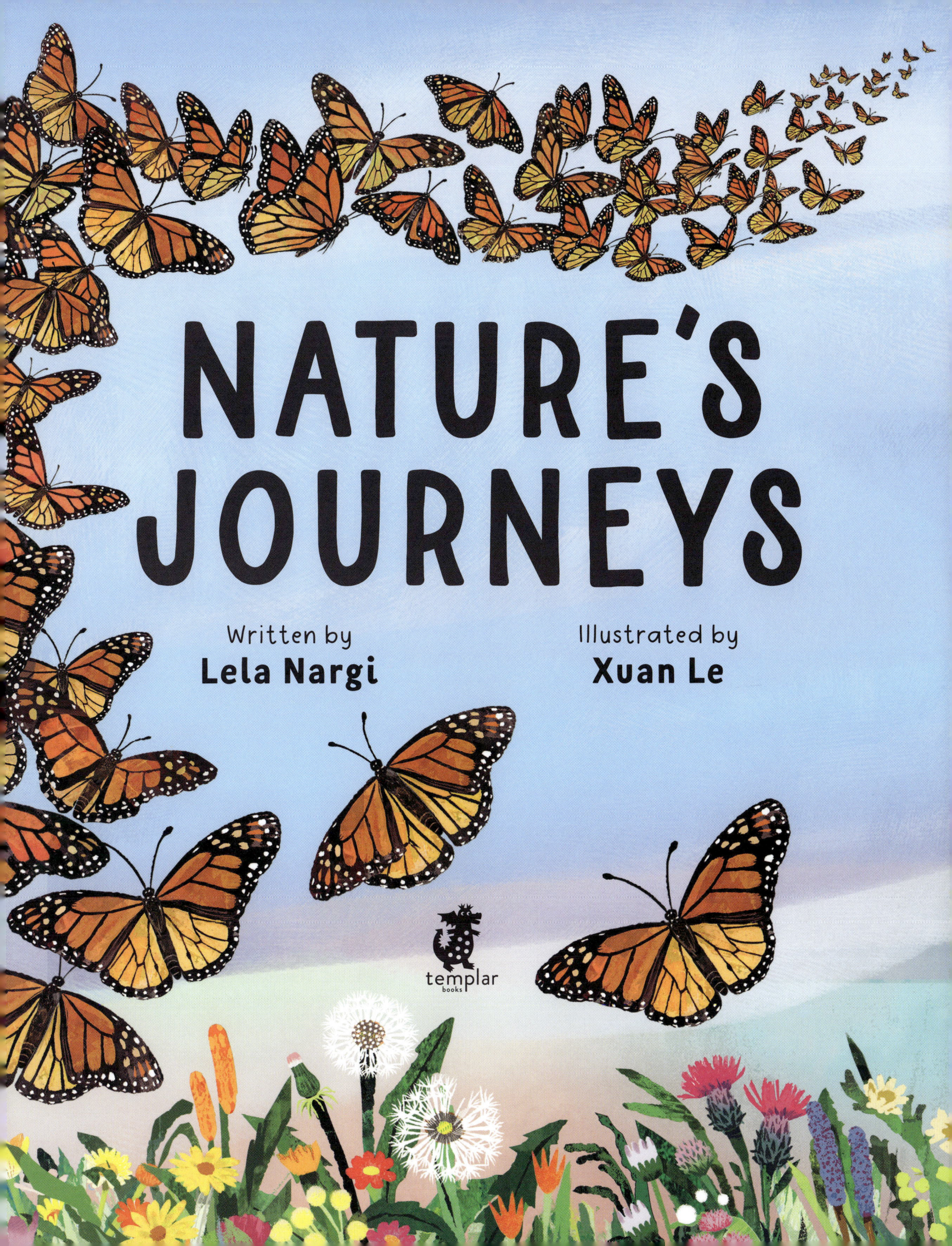

The wind comes.
It is movement with a purpose.
It blows rain clouds across the sky and helps life drift to new places.

Wind happens when the Sun heats the Earth's surface. As the Earth spins around the Sun, it heats more in some places and less in others. In hot spots, air rises. In cool spots, air falls. When hot and cool air mix together, you get wind. Our planet's wind cycle blows rain clouds across the sky, which helps move water around our planet in the water cycle.

The water cycle works like this: the Sun heats water on the Earth's surface and turns it into VAPOUR. This vapour rises to form clouds...

When clouds become heavy with water, they drop it back to Earth as rain or snow...

But everything that goes must also stop. This gives life a chance to settle and cling.

Raindrops and snowflakes soak into soil, fill up lakes and fall into rivers that flow back into the ocean. Then the water cycle starts all over again.

The wind snatches ash from the plume of an erupting volcano. It carries these tiny specks of rock and glass up and up to drift with the clouds.

Hot liquid rock, called magma, burbles deep inside the Earth. Volcanoes spit it out onto land, and then it is known as lava.

Some volcanoes, such as Mount Etna in Italy, blast lava out with such force that it turns instantly to ash and rises high into the atmosphere. Other volcanoes erupt gently, oozing out rivers of lava.

Lots of animals thrive near active volcanoes.

Some ash bits cling together,
now too heavy to drift very far.
They fall down and down,
blanketing the land.

An ash plume may drift for thousands of kilometres or even circle the globe.

Ash can pile up so deeply on the ground that it buries whole towns.

As it breaks down over time, volcanic ash releases MINERALS into the soil. This rich soil then feeds crops like olives and grapes. This is why so many farms and vineyards are planted at the foot of volcanoes.

The wind riffles the grass as spiderlings climb to the tops of stalks. They shoot silk into the air to parachute to new meadows.

Spiders have glands in their abdomens that produce liquid silk. When they push this liquid through their SPINNERETS, it turns to thread. These threads catch the wind to help some spiders become airborne. It's a mode of travel called 'ballooning'. Some ballooning spiders can jet for hundreds of kilometres.

Tiny golden orb weaver spiderlings balloon a few days after hatching from their egg sac. This lets them spread out so they can all find enough food.

When the spiders land, they spin sticky webs to catch tasty insect prey.

Female African social velvet spiders balloon as adults. They release silk threads that form triangle-shaped silk sails that carry them off to find new mates.

Crab spiders have tiny hairs on their legs that are covered with even tinier hairs called setules. These help them cling to surfaces when they land.

Western monarchs travel from California to Canada.

When they reach their destinations, they are ready to make the next generation of butterflies.

They lay their eggs, fastening them to leaves with a special goo.

A caterpillar has six legs and up to ten PROLEGS — fleshy leg-like structures with tiny hooks that help them cling to stems and leaves.

When a caterpillar is ready to become a butterfly, it forms a hard outer casing called a chrysalis. It then attaches itself to a leaf or twig using silk threads.

On the Alaskan coast, the wind lifts tundra swans as they fly against it. It holds kestrels perfectly still in a hover.

A kestrel hovers by flying into wind at the same speed the wind is moving.

Tundra swans run on water while they flap into the wind. The rush of air lifts their heavy bodies.

Black-footed albatrosses ride the wind like a rollercoaster, soaring for hundreds of kilometres without flapping their huge wings. They fly into fast-moving air to go up and slow-moving air to plunge down. This is called DYNAMIC SOARING.

Albatrosses soar over enire oceans. Sooner or later each of these birds drifts back to land.

Songbirds cling with perching feet as the breeze ruffles their feathers.

Songbirds like the yellow-rumped warbler have three toes that face the front and one toe that faces back. They use these to tightly grip onto branches.

The hot summer wind rises. It scatters sand across the steppe that it has carried here from the desert.

Tumbleweeds start as Russian thistle bushes. They are native to the Eurasian STEPPE, a grassland that stretches from Hungary to Mongolia. In one year, thistles grow, die and pull away from the soil. Wind blows them hundreds of kilometres over land, scattering their many seeds.

It skitters tumbleweeds across the plains. It scoops up dandelion and maple seeds.

Maple seeds nestle in pods called SAMARAS. These pods act like propellers, whirling away on a breeze.

A dandelion seed is attached to a plume of hairs called a PAPPUS. It catches the wind like a sail.

But not all seeds need the wind to move. Some hitch rides on passing animals.

Some seeds cling with hooks or spines. Cockleburs catch a lift on squirrels and rabbits, tangled in their fur.

Throughout Europe, grazing sheep may become covered in narrow-leaf clover, wild carrot and hare's foot plantain seeds. They brush off the animals' coats and land in soil.

And not all plants need to grow in soil. In a rainforest, they coil their roots around other plants and bark for support.

The Chilean pitcher flower is an EPIPHYTE found in the cool rainforests of Chile. Epiphytes make their homes on other plants. They take water not from the ground but straight from the humid air.

Spanish moss has no roots at all. This tropical epiphyte hangs onto branches with tiny scales called trichomes.

Something else clings to these clinging plants. Look close.

There are 8,000 species of parasitic bugs called scale insects. They are covered by a waxy or powdery coating that sticks them to plants so they can suck out their sap.

Orchids have hair-covered roots that let them hold tight onto a host tree. Their roots are also spongy, which helps them to absorb water.

The scent of their flowers wafts through the trees, luring orchid bees.

Strangler fig trees start out as epiphytes. But once their roots touch the ground, they become PARASITES and slowly strangle their host trees!

Animals cling to trees, too. High up in the Amazon's canopy, the leaves furry bodies hide amongst.

Mushrooms like this bracket fungus release their microscopic SPORES into the air to reproduce. Spores also attract water drops as they drift, helping to create rain clouds.

A three-toed sloth has hook-shaped claws, perfect for hanging from branches. When climbing up a tree, these dig into the bark, similar to the way a woodpecker uses its sharp toes to cling.

A kinkajou uses its PREHENSILE tail to hang from tree branches. It reaches for food with its hands and slurps it with its extra-long tongue!

These creatures have special features to help secure them.

Drifting past them on a gentle wind are tiny fungus spores, catching rides to grow in new places.

Gusts of wind scatter maple samaras far from their mother tree, past a place where land meets ocean.

Here, mangroves grip soft mud with their tall stilt roots as they're battered by waves.

Mangroves are hardy trees that are native to places like Okinawa, Japan. They have special roots that grow up into the air, like snorkels, letting the trees breathe underwater.

Mangrove tree crabs live in the mud beneath the trees, feeding on dropped leaves.

When this maple seed lands in rich soil, it will send roots deep into the earth. The roots of maple trees grow sideways. They can reach three times further than their branches.

The waves carry baby mangroves into the shallows, where they take root and start to grow.

Red mangrove trees grow long green seed pods called PROPAGULES. These sprout while they are still attached to the mother tree. Then they break off and drift on currents to take root somewhere new.

An adult mangrove's roots act as a protective nursery for fish like snappers and pufferfish.

The wind ripples the surface of rivers and estuaries. It pushes floating seeds towards the ocean.

'Sea beans' or 'drift seeds' are seeds that fall into rivers, then make their way to the ocean. They can drift for years and thousands of kilometres, kept afloat by air pockets inside their shells.

The South Equatorial Current carries 'sea hearts', the seeds of a flowering vine, from West Africa to Texas, USA. Up to 15 of these heart-shaped seeds grow in each giant pod.

The North Equatorial Current picks up sea mango seeds from the Pacific islands and drops them on beaches in Japan. Sea mango trees produce fruit that is pretty — and poisonous!

The wind helps ocean currents form. These powerful flows move nutrients and heat around the globe.

Across the ocean, the wind becomes a gale, swirling the water into currents. They snatch up the seeds and set them sailing.

The Gulf Stream brings grey nickernuts from the Caribbean across the North Atlantic Ocean to Scotland. Grey nicker plants grow like vines on mangrove trees. Their spiky green fruit pods split open to drop their seeds into water.

By-the-wind sailors are jellyfish-like animals. They drift with ocean currents, using their 'sail' to catch the wind.

The East Australian Current carries candlenuts from Australia to New Zealand. Candlenut trees produce oily nuts that can be burned to make light.

Along the coast, strong winds and tides pull dead trees and branches out to sea, as if they were light as feathers.

Trees growing beside rivers often fall in when they die and get pulled out to sea, becoming DRIFTWOOD. They may travel ocean currents for a year or more.

Some driftwood may sink to the bottom of the ocean. There, it rots to feed marine life on the sea floor like bacteria and worms.

Maybe, one day, they will reach a distant shore. In the woody holes of these stumps are castaways hitching rides.

In northern parts of the world, tiny crustaceans called driftwood hoppers, a type of TALITRID, move into holes in driftwood. Here, they live their whole lives, even raising their young at sea. Driftwood hoppers may get eaten if their home joins a floating reef. These are island-like masses of tangled wood where fish, such as tuna, and birds, such as pelicans, take shelter in the ocean.

Waves crash against rocks near the shore. The wind scatters the spray and pulls it skyward.

The mussels that cling in the cracks do not budge...

Green-lipped mussels are MOLLUSCS that live in New Zealand. They cling to rocks using stretchy cords with glue-y tips, called BYSSUS THREADS.

but the ocean currents draw out their larvae and propel them towards forests of kelp.

After drifting, mussel larvae, known as SPAT, attach to kelp. If they don't like the taste of the kelp, they let go and balloon to another spot using a long thread of mucus.

Skate eggs, called mermaid purses, also cling to kelp. That's what the four hooks on their cases are for.

Kelp is seaweed that holds fast to the ocean floor with root-like strings known as HOLDFASTS. Their leaves have air pockets that make them float upright.

Those same currents sway strands of seaweed that hold cargoes of eel eggs.

Sargassum is brown seaweed from the Sargasso Sea in the Atlantic Ocean. Air pockets on its stems help it float in thick mats on the water's surface. Currents wash it onto beaches in parts of the United States, Europe and Africa.

Both American and European eels live most of their lives in rivers on their home continents. As adults, they travel to the Sargasso Sea to lay their eggs.

When the eggs hatch they drift to distant rivers.

The seaweed floats to shore, where it dries and dies and nourishes beach plants.

Their eggs hatch into larvae that ride the currents back to Europe or North America. They grow as they go — first into glass eels that reach rivers when they are a year old. Then they become elvers, then yellow eels, then silver eels. Adult silver eels swim back to the Sargasso Sea to spawn, starting the life cycle all over again.

The ocean is snowing! Flakes sparkle in the sunlight near the surface. Slowly, they drift down into the dark depths.

Marine snow is made up of sand, as well as dead animals and plants that are now rotted to dust. Just like volcanic ash, it contains nutrients. Just like sunken driftwood, it brings those nutrients to fish and deep-sea creatures such as vampire squid.

What eel larvae eat was a mystery to scientists for a long time. But now we know they eat the most nutritious bits of marine snow. This helps them grow and store energy.

They grow bigger as they fall,
clinging together and falling faster.

Still, the long trip
to the ocean floor
takes many weeks.

The vampire squid is gentle, despite its name. It reaches out sticky filaments from its body to catch marine snow, and its arms scrape these morsels into its mouth.

Marine snow that isn't eaten settles on the ocean floor. There, it holds and stores carbon, playing an important role in keeping our planet cool and liveable.

In the midst of this watery snowfall even the biggest animals drift. Most whales travel the ocean in an endless search for food.

Barnacles are crustaceans, like crabs. As larvae, they float in currents. They make a cement-like substance to attach themselves to rocks, turtles or baleen whales and cling there for their whole lives. They eat the PLANKTON that they collect with their feathery legs.

Sometimes barnacles travel with them. Latched onto whales' bodies, these little crustaceans gather food from the water.

When it's time to rest, these gentle giants drift to sleep, suspended beneath the waves.

There are five major currents in the ocean, known as GYRES. Many migrating animals travel on these ocean 'highways' to search for food. Some whales travel a million kilometres in their lifetimes.

Baleen whales, like blue whales, eat mostly krill and other tiny animals. Toothed whales, like sperm whales, eat squid and fish living in deep water.

When sperm whales sleep they drift dive, floating upright with their heads near the water's surface and their bodies dangling down.

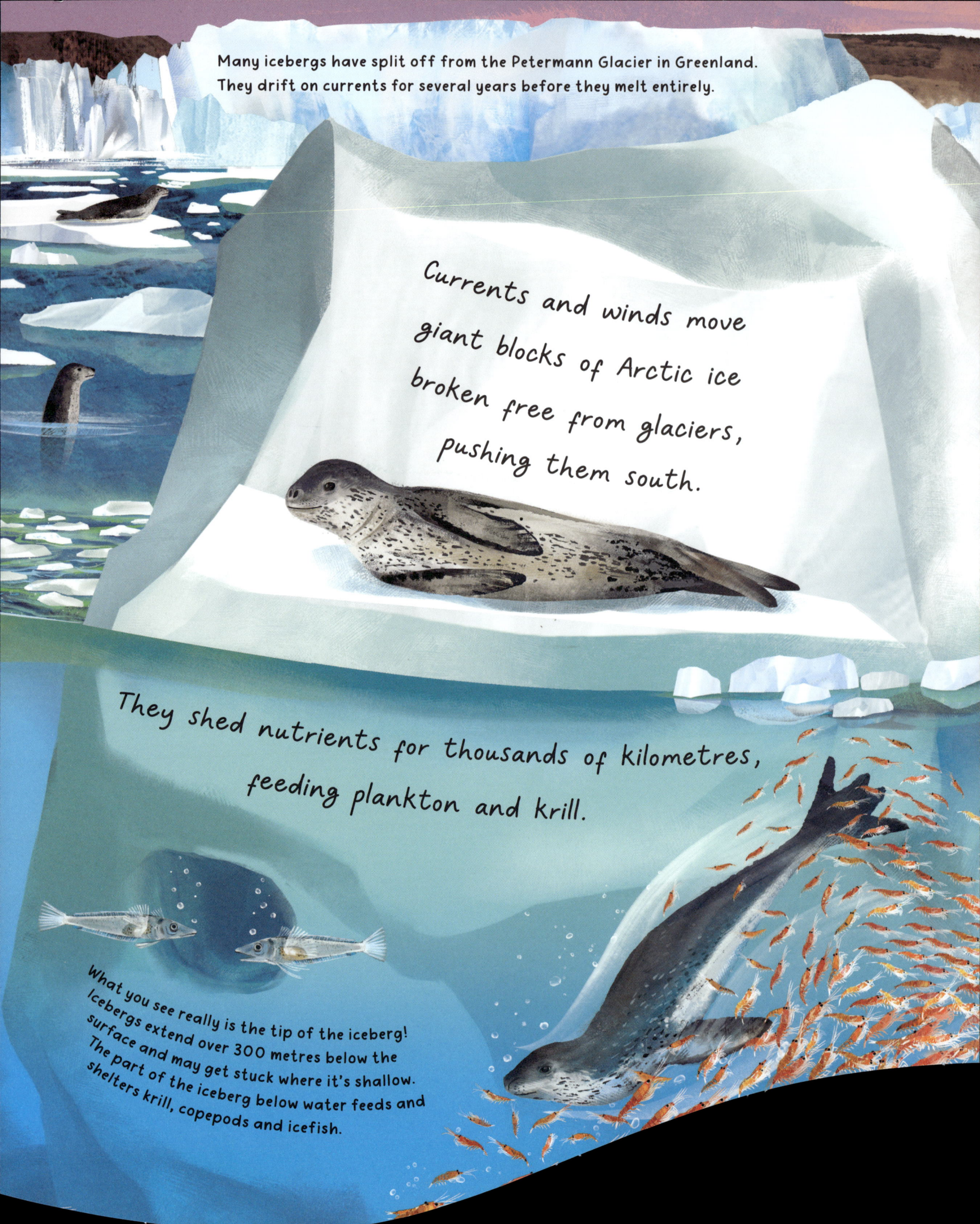

Many icebergs have split off from the Petermann Glacier in Greenland. They drift on currents for several years before they melt entirely.

Currents and winds move giant blocks of Arctic ice broken free from glaciers, pushing them south.

They shed nutrients for thousands of kilometres, feeding plankton and krill.

What you see really is the tip of the iceberg! Icebergs extend over 300 metres below the surface and may get stuck where it's shallow. The part of the iceberg below water feeds and shelters krill, copepods and icefish.

All the minerals that shed off an iceberg feed bacteria, algae, krill and copepods — which are tasty snacks for fish. In turn, fish are eaten by petrels, harbour seals and polar bears.

Whales, sea turtles and jellyfish follow in the icebergs' trails to enjoy the feast.

Icebergs fertilise the ocean as they travel. They are dusted with dark sand, called cryoconite, that is blown more than 6,000 kilometres from the Gobi Desert. The sand heats up in the Sun to melt nutrients like iron and oxygen into the water.

Jellyfish drift past anemones and sea sponges that cling to icebergs, rocks, reefs — and even crabs.

Anemones gobble up jellyfish for a snack. Yum!

Some people think jellyfish only drift. But these INVERTEBRATES can sense currents and swim both with and against them.

Most anemones are shaped like columns. One end of the column is a mouth. The other end contains a slimy foot, called a PEDAL DISC, that sticks to surfaces.

Bits of sea sponge break off, then they drift, too.

They will settle again when they find a new home to stick onto.

Sea sponges live on the sea floor. They anchor themselves with tiny strong hairs made of glass, called SPICULES, that crust onto a rocky surface. There they stay, eating plankton that they filter out from the water.

Sea sponges reproduce in three ways. They grow buds that break off and grow into new sponges. Or they break off pieces of themselves that attach to new surfaces and grow into new sponges. Or they lay eggs, then produce sperm to fertilise the eggs that mature into a new crop of sponges.

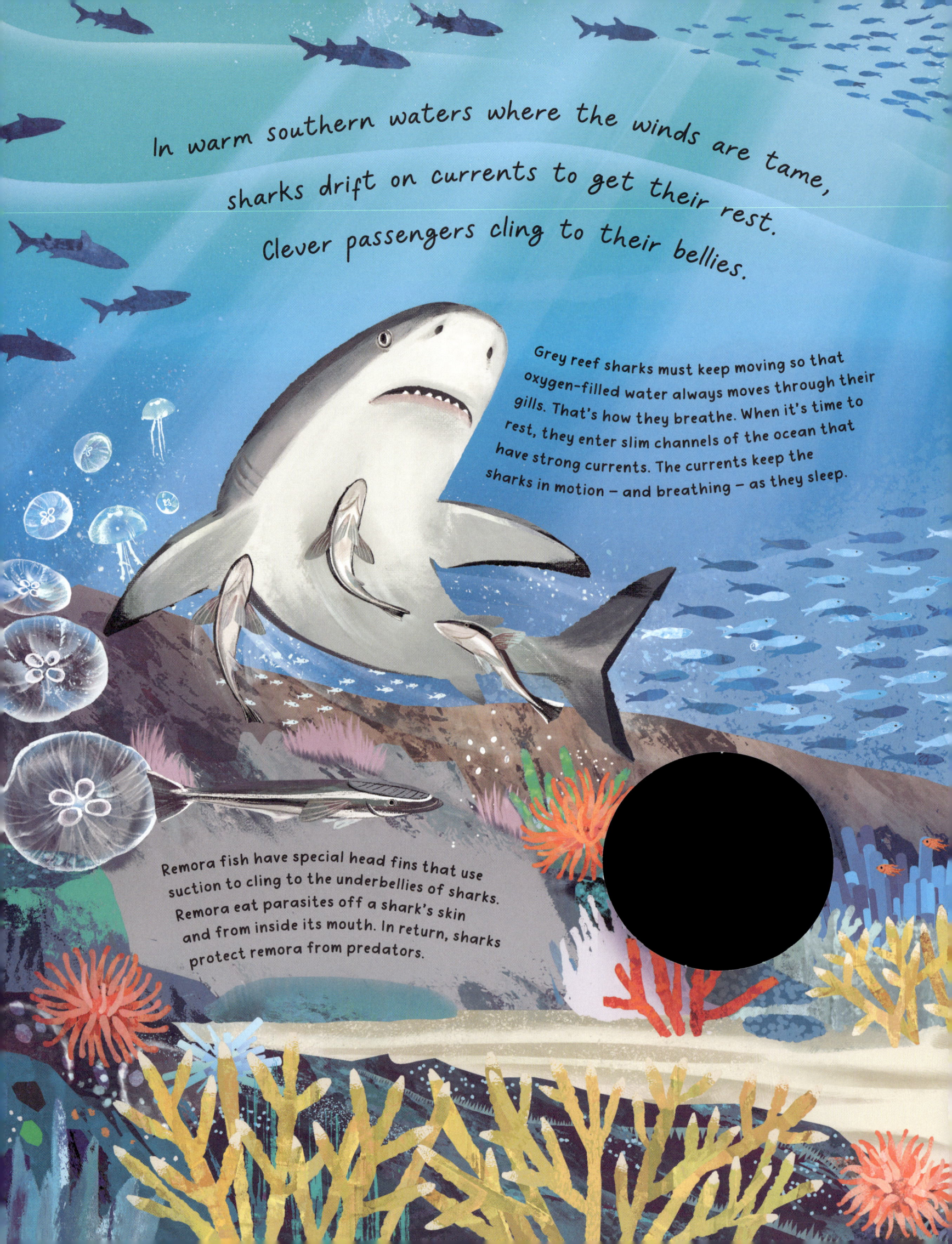

In warm southern waters where the winds are tame, sharks drift on currents to get their rest. Clever passengers cling to their bellies.

Grey reef sharks must keep moving so that oxygen-filled water always moves through their gills. That's how they breathe. When it's time to rest, they enter slim channels of the ocean that have strong currents. The currents keep the sharks in motion — and breathing — as they sleep.

Remora fish have special head fins that use suction to cling to the underbellies of sharks. Remora eat parasites off a shark's skin and from inside its mouth. In return, sharks protect remora from predators.

Other creatures are not so lucky. They find themselves inside a shark's huge mouth instead.

The whale shark is the largest fish species. It swims slowly near the water's surface with its mouth open, filtering out plankton and small fish through its sieve-like GILL RAKERS.

Their drifting has come to an end. All around them the rest of the world drifts on.

Some shark species, such as nurse sharks and wobbegongs, rest or 'sit' on the sea floor. They use their pectoral fins to prop themselves up.

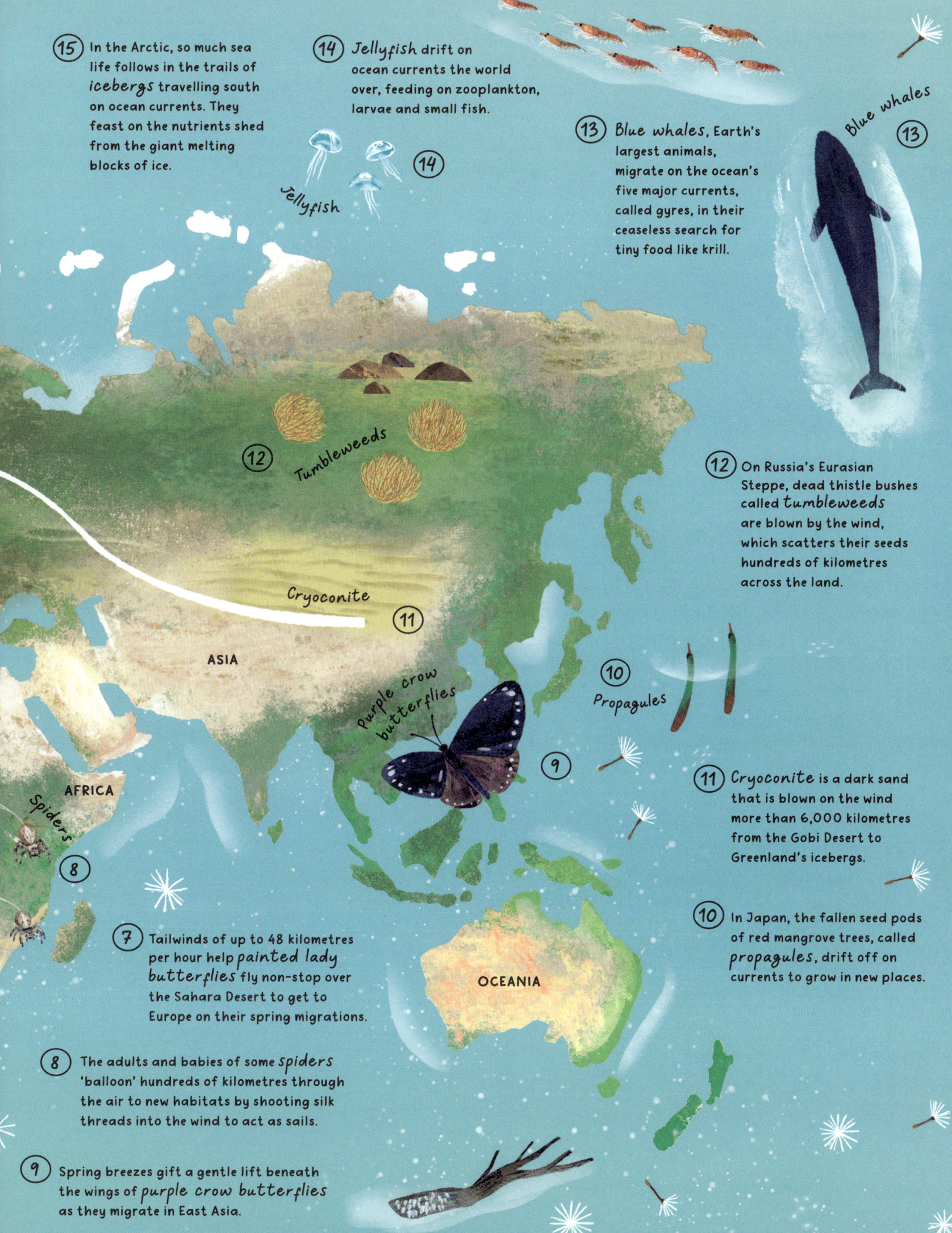

GLOSSARY

BYSSUS THREAD:
A strong, stretchy cord made by glands in a mollusc's 'foot'. Several byssus threads help attach the animal to surfaces.

DRIFTWOOD:
Dead trees and branches that drift into the ocean and travel on currents and tides.

DYNAMIC SOARING:
A way of gliding that lets albatrosses fly great distances on the wind without flapping.

EPIPHYTE:
A plant that grows on a host plant instead of in soil. It gets moisture from rain or water vapour and nutrients from dead plant matter.

GILL RAKER:
An extra comb-like part inside the gills of some fish. Gill rakers allow fish to filter tiny bits of food, like plankton, from the water.

GYRE:
A circular system of ocean currents that are moved by wind.

HOLDFAST:
A disc that grows from seaweed to help it cling to rocks. Also known as a hapteron.

INVERTEBRATE:
An animal that has no backbone.

MINERAL:
Non-living stuff that usually comes from rocks. Salt, iron and gold are all minerals.

MOLLUSC:
An animal with a soft body covered by a mantle. Usually this mantle is a hard shell. Clams, snails and squid are molluscs.

PAPPUS:
The tufty bit on dandelion and other seeds that helps them catch the wind and travel.

PARASITE:
A living thing that lives on or in another living thing, feeding on it and causing it harm.

PEDAL DISC:
The non-mouth end of an anemone that secretes a sticky film to stick to wet surfaces.

PLANKTON:
Tiny floating water organisms that are eaten by many larger organisms. Phytoplankton are algae while zooplankton are small animals.

PREHENSILE:
Animals such as monkeys have prehensile tails or limbs. These can wrap around an object, such as a branch, to hold onto it.

PROLEG:
A stubby hind leg on a caterpillar used for walking and clinging. A caterpillar has six front 'true' legs as well as up to ten prolegs.

PROPAGULE:
A seed, bud or other plant growth that falls off and grows into a new plant.

SAMARA:
A wing-shaped seed pod, like those of the maple tree.

SPAT:
Young shellfish in their larval form.

SPICULE:
One of the tiny needle-like crystals that form the skeletons of many sponges. Some sponges also use spicules to anchor themselves.

SPINNERET:
The silk-spinning organ of a spider and some insects.

SPORE:
A tiny seed-like speck that fungi, bacteria and some plants release to reproduce.

STEPPE:
A grassland with few or no trees.

TAILWIND:
A wind that blows at you from behind, in the direction you're going. As opposed to a headwind, which blows against you.

TALITRID:
A type of invertebrate in the Talitridae family, which lives on the shore in seaweed or at sea in driftwood.

VAPOUR:
A substance, such as water, in its gas form.